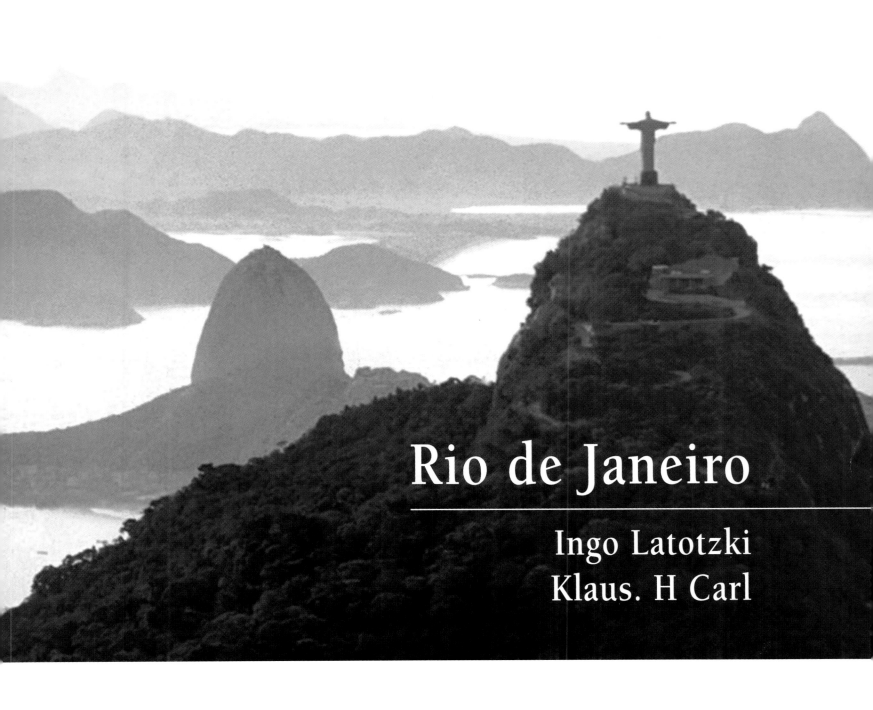

Rio de Janeiro

Ingo Latotzki
Klaus. H Carl

Publishing Director : Jean-Paul Manzo
Text : Ingo Latotzki
Design: Cédric Pontes
Layout: Sébastien Ceste

We would like to extend special thanks to Mike Darton for his invaluable cooperation

We are very grateful to the Rio Tourist Office in Paris and to the Bresilian Tourist Office in London.

Photograph credits :
© Ricardo Azoury / Brazilian Tourist Office in London : ill. P. 1, 4; ill. 9, 10, 11, 14, 15, 23, 24, 25, 30, 41, 42, 45, 48, 55, 60, 62, 63, 64, 69, 81, 82, 83, 86, 93, 94, 96, 97, 98, 99, 100, 101, 104, 105, 106, 107, 108, 111, 112, 113, 114, 115, 116, 117, 118, 119, 120, 121, 122.
© Klaus H.Carl : ill. 12, 13, 16, 17, 18, 19, 20, 21, 22, 32, 33, 35, 36, 37, 44, 46, 49, 50, 51, 52, 53, 54, 58, 61, 65, 66, 71, 73,74,75 , 76, 77, 78, 79, 80, 84, 85, 87, 88, 89, 90, 91, 95, 102, 103, 109, 110
© Sue Cunningham Photographic : ill. 26, 27, 28, 29, 31, 34, 38, 39, 40, 47, 56, 57, 59, 67, 68, 70, 72,
© J.Valliot : 43.

Rio de Janeiro

Ingo Latotzki

Contents

The arrival of the Portuguese
The founding of Rio

The story goes that it was on the morning of New Year's day 1502 that the Florentine merchant-navigator Amerigo Vespucci made an uncharacteristic error of judgement – and so gave Rio de Janeiro its name. Vespucci was on a voyage of exploration, thought the wide Guanabara Bay was the estuary of some large river, and so called the whole area Rio de Janeiro, 'January River'.

It was only two years earlier that the Portuguese explorer Pedro Alves Cabral had discovered and laid claim to the whole of Brazil. For some decades thereafter, however, the sugar plantations in the north of the territory were the main focus for colonization. The Portuguese during this time left the more southerly areas to their own devices – and to the incursions of the French, who seized the region (and renamed it La France Antarctique).

So it was not until 1565 that the Portuguese finally decided to enforce their control. They founded their own settlement (which they called São Sebastião do Rio de Janeiro in honour of King Sebastian of Portugal) and evicted the French. Development of Rio was slow, even then. The harbour was small and rather open. The more northerly provinces remained of more colonial value.

Then suddenly, at the end of the 17th century, gold was discovered in the neighboring province of Minas Gerais. Rio's fortunes changed overnight as a gold rush started. Thousands of prospectors – mostly from Portugal – descended on Rio, and a road was hastily built from there all the way out to the goldfields. Together with the prospectors came all kinds of other hangers-on, and the settlement expanded hugely in all directions. Rio became the center for shipping Brazilian gold back to Portugal, and Portugal soon became one of Europe's richest nations. This is how Rio became a major economic hub in the astoundingly vast country that is Brazil.

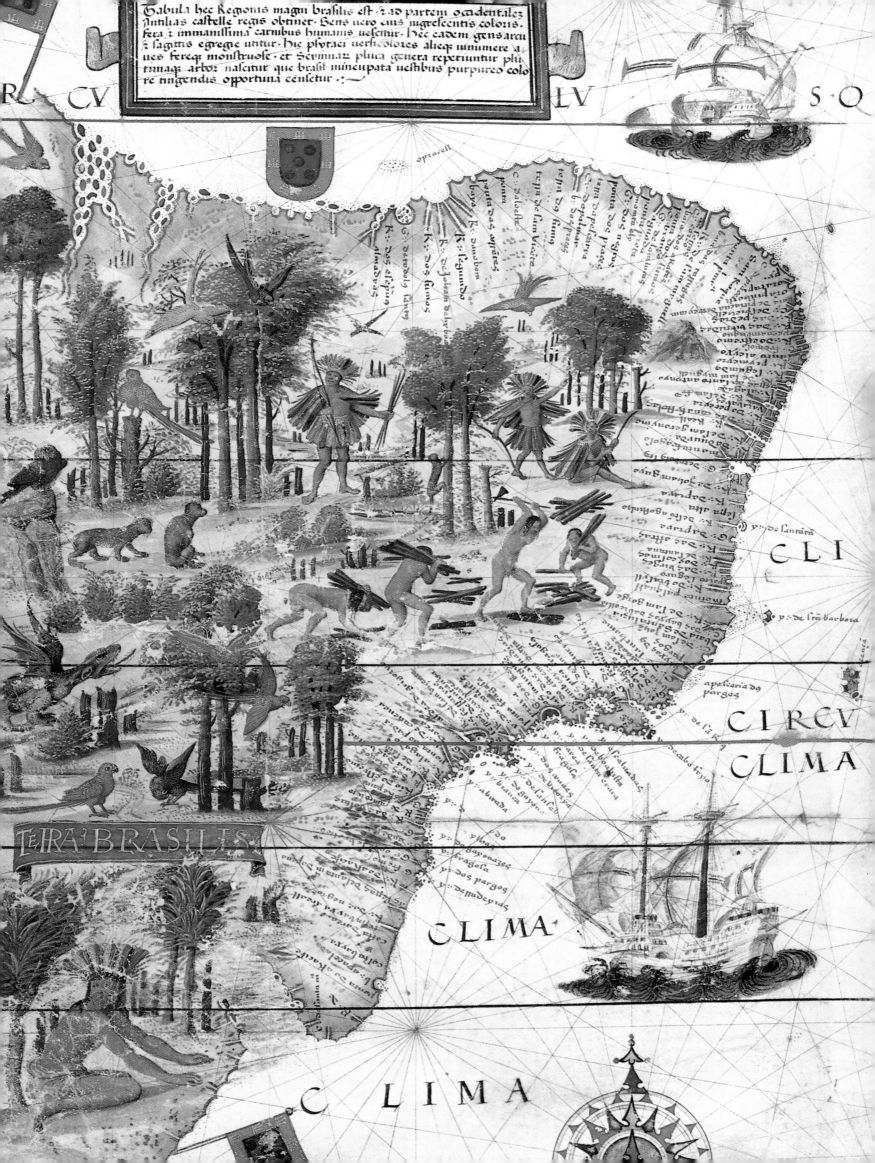

Tabula hec Regionis magni brasilis est: ad partem occidentalez
Antillas castelle regis obtinet. Gens uero eius nigrescentis coloris.
fera: z immanissima carnibus humanis uescitur. Hec eadem gens arcu
z sagittis egregie untur. Hic psittaci uersicolores aliaq; innumere a
ues fereq; monstruose. et Seminaz plura genera reperiuntur plu
rimaq; arbor nascitur que brasil nuncupata uestibus purpureo colo
re tingendis opportuna censetur.

RV   CV   LV   S O

CLI

CIRCV

CLIMA

CLIMA·

TERRA·BRASILIS

CLIMA

1 The arrival of Pedro Alves Cabral on April 22,1500. Oscar Pereira da Silva. Museum of National History, Rio de Janeiro.

2 The road out to the goldfields.

3 Map of Brazil dating from 1519.

4 Peasant farmers delivering coffee beans to the local foreman.

5 Growing sugar cane.

6 A portrait of the Regent John (Dom João VI).

7 A portrait of Dom Pedro I.

8 The arrival of Getúlio Vargas in Rio de Janeiro.

For a while the city even became the seat of the Portuguese regency court, after the regent John (Dom João VI) had been obliged to quit Portugal in 1808 with some 15,000 of the Portuguese aristocracy. Once more Rio expanded massively. Schools and banks were built. Parks were laid out. The place had its own newspapers. Rio looked increasingly like a European city.

More important, though, was the regent's decision to open up the city to forms of trade previously restricted to Portugal. The result was a thunderous economic boom. Rio took on world trade status. Dom João returned to Portugal in 1821, by which time the city had more than 100,000 residents – three times as many as when he had arrived 13 years before. He left his son, Dom Pedro, behind to govern the colony. The following year, however, under the influence of Brazilian nationalists, Brazil declared independence with Dom Pedro as its first 'emperor' and Rio as its first national capital. The city's growth continued on in ever more modern a guise. In 1854 its streets were lit by gas lamps. In 1874 the telegraph connected Rio with London.

The good times could not go on for ever. Rich landowners seized political power and divided the nation's main sources of revenue between themselves. They also hired and fired the country's presidents. It was not until 1930 that Getúlio Vargas engineered a coup and finally brought down the land-owning class. Popular government was now the aim: it was the will of the people that was important. Yet more significantly it was the number of the people that was growing, especially in Rio, where space was at a premium amongst congested overbuilding. The city began to sprawl at the edges, inching southward along the beaches.

The congestion had really begun more than two decades earlier – around the time the central boulevard (Avenida Centra) had been constructed through the city in 1905. Then, high-rise buildings were put up, some with 30 stories or more. Living space became ultra-cramped. This was a problem that the city of São Paulo, 225 miles (350 kilometers) southwest of Rio, did not suffer from. And indeed, in 1959 São Paulo surpassed Rio in terms both of annual revenue and of total population. The final and worst humiliation for Rio came in 1960, when President Juscelino Kubitschek moved the seat of government from Rio to the new city of Brasília. For a long and painful period this caused the citizens of Rio to search for a new identity. Since then, more and more industrial jobs have been lost to the south, although Rio continues to attract poorer migrants who straggle in from the northeast and from the interior of the country. They swell the numbers in the favelas and slum tenements at the northern edge of the city.

Something else that affected Rio badly was that the city's own state municipality was governed by politicians opposed to the military leaders of Brazil who ruled the country between 1965 and 1985. In consequence, for twenty years Rio received far fewer financial allocations than other cities.

But more recently things have been looking up. Oil deposits have been detected offshore, and the resultant wealth has flowed into the city. A proportion of the money has been spent on urban renovation. This has not stopped some of the locals from being sardonic. They say, darkly, that the decisions may now be made in Brasília or in São Paulo – but the plots are hatched in Rio.

This is a development Amerigo Vespucci could certainly not have foreseen when he – the first tourist visitor, you might say – beheld the wide blue Guanabara Bay.

«God created Rio on a Sunday»

The city that never sleeps

9. Aerial view of the city.

10. View of the mountains. In the distance is the statue of Christ the Redeemer.

11. View of São Conrado.

First impressions of Rio for the air traveler are of scale. A vista of bays surrounded by mountains; an incredibly crowded mass of buildings and roads; sandy beaches lining a tortuously long shore. And then the statue of Christ the Redeemer on top of Corcovado mountain. For some visitors from the United States, this is reminiscent of New York and the Statue of Liberty when approached from the air. It is almost as if the mayor of the city has come out personally to greet you, say no few of the tourists on seeing the mighty figure shortly before they land.

Cristo Redentor, Christ the Redeemer, is one of Rio's best-known landmarks. A colossal structure, it is $98^{1/2}$ feet (30 meters) high, weighs about 1,000 tons, and was sculpted by the Frenchman Paul Landowski following the design of the Brazilian engineer Heitor Silva Costa. It took him five years. The figure's widest span is nearly 92 feet (28 meters). Each of the hands measures $10^{1/2}$ feet (3.2 meters) across and weighs no less than 8 tons. The base of the statue of Christ is already at an altitude of 2,310 feet (704 meters) above the level of the sea below. In the mornings, after the sea-mist has lifted and the sun bathes all in oranges and reds, the statue makes a compelling subject for photos. Even later in the day it remains truly spectacular. Some 800,000 tourists a year come to marvel at it. Recently restored (at a cost of several million dollars), the statue at night is illuminated from below in a greenish-white light.

But Rio offers a great number of spectacular views. Some of the finest panoramas of the city are from the surrounding mountains, of which there are many. Yet Rio is naturally beautiful too. As Charles Darwin wrote at the beginning of the 19th century when he visited the area, 'In its majestic beauty, Guanabara Bay surpasses any area of natural beauty visible by Europeans in their home countries.' The teeming city, now with 10 million residents, has changed since then, of course, but most of its attractive elements remain the same as ever. Rio is well worth seeing. The inhabitants of Rio state categorically that God must be Brazilian, and that He created the Earth in six days and on the seventh He created Rio – the city on the January River. These are expressions that people from elsewhere in the world use about their own home cities, their own countries – but they do demonstrate the emotion involved.

Pão de Açúcar, the Sugarloaf mountain, is another sight classic to Rio – one of the most instantly recognizable views in the world. Three different vistas, all spectacular, are laid before the eyes of those who climb the 1,296-feet (395-meter) high mountain. One is of the curving gulf that is the Botafogo Inlet to the west; another is of the 9-mile (14-kilometer) long Rio–Niterói Bridge to the east; and the third – if the sky is clear enough – is of the peaks of the Serra Flumenense, about an hour's drive up the freeway from Rio.

12. The statue of Christ the Redeemer from a medium distance.

13. View of the city, with Corcovado ('the Hunchback') and the Sugarloaf mountain.

14. The bridge between Rio and Niterói.

Rio's newest Catholic cathedral, São Sebastião, stands at no great distance from the impressive Petrobras tower. Local architect Oliveira Fondseca based his design for the cathedral on a Mexican pyramid. Some observers have unkindly likened it instead to an upturned flowerpot. It is undoubtedly a futuristic building. Able to accommodate almost 2,000 worshipers, it was consecrated in 1976. Its campanile stands adjacent. The cathedral's most glorious occasion to date happened in 1991, when Pope John II celebrated mass there to a total congregation of 20,000 mustered inside and outside the building.

But back to the secular and profane. Visitors find that it can take rather more than a couple of days to be able to see all the major tourists sites in Rio. One special way of getting about, though, is to use the more-than-a-hundred-year-old streetcar service from the town center to Santa Teresa. Only this stretch is left of the tracks today, but in the 1960s more than 250 miles (400 kilometers) of track were in daily use. Don't take this as any kind of recommendation, but the best views are to be seen from the streetcar's running-boards (a vantage-point that costs nothing extra except audacity and agility). The streetcar climbs laboriously all the way to Santa Teresa, groaning and rattling over the cobblestones. This part of the city is now home mostly to artists and retains many of its original villas and houses built in high Victorian style.

35. The front of São Sebastião Cathedral.

36. Stained-glass windows seen from inside the new cathedral.

37. Crypt in São Sebastião Cathedral.

38. The Petrobras headquarters
    building.
39. Petrobras research
    buildings.
40. Detail of the architecture
    of the Petrobras building.

41. Ilha do Fiscal.
42. The Botanical Gardens.
43. An orchid.
44. Sculpture in a park.

45. The arched aqueduct of Lapa.

46. Tramway for the streetcars.

In recent times two architects have had major influences on buildings in Rio: Oscar Niemeyer and Roberto Burle Marx. Niemeyer has probably designed more buildings in the city than anybody else. His personal style is characterized by bold effects, especially sweeping curves. It was he who was responsible for the celebrated Sambodrom, approximately half a mile (800 meters) long with seats arranged in stadium format, and for the large sculpture at one end. He also designed the Museum of Contemporary Art in Niterói which opened in 1996, and which is considered by many to be the most forward-looking construction in all of Rio. Built on a rocky promontory above the ocean, the museum looks not unlike a huge white flower. It features a façade incorporating thermal fabric developed by NASA, and windows with glass nearly an inch (2 centimeters) thick, able to withstand hurricanes of up to Force 16 on the Beaufort scale. From here, sightseers have an excellent 180-degree view of Rio, the Sugarloaf, and Corcovado. The building is itself artistically illuminated at night.

Burle Marx, who died in 1994, was more of a landscape artist. He had a hand in the design of many of the parks and gardens in

47. View of the harbour from
Santa Teresa.

Rio. On his death he bequeathed his home at Guaratiba, a small fishing-village to the southwest, to the city. The number and variety of tropical plants in his garden surpasses those in the collection of Rio's own official botanical gardens. Visible from the house is an extensive mangrove swamp, impressive in its natural scenery. Similarly to the south are some peaceful spots around Grumari. Beaches, granite boulders, clear warm water – what could be better for a quick stop-off on our tour of discovery through Rio de Janeiro?

Somewhere else well worth the visit is the Confeitaria Colombo, a restaurant and coffee-house located right in the middle of downtown Rio, and looking as if it had come straight from Paris in the 1890s. The coffee-house is indeed more than 100 years old, built in Portuguese colonial style. Inside, the décor is rich, featuring rosewood paneling and Italian marble. The tea-room (salão de chá) on the first floor may be the best place to enjoy the pleasantly unusual ambiance. And also to indulge in a snack – some cake, maybe, or some tasty ice cream.

48. The Santa Teresa district.

49. Monument to General
    Osorio in the old town.
50. Crypt in the Church of São
    Bento in the old town.
51. Fire-station in the old town.

Refreshed and fortified, then is the time to continue on to perhaps the most beautiful of all Rio's museums: the Casa do Pontal. It is actually a museum of everyday life – especially the everyday lives of the poor – and in its way is more illustrative of history than any historical or sociological reference book could be. Glass cabinets contain masses of miniature figures all in appropriate costume and surrounded by their habitual environments. Samba dancers, day-laborers, drunkards in bars, plantation workers, poor migrants looking for work or for shelter, even the occasional saint. Around 3,000 in all, they are mostly the work of various native Brazilians from the northeast of the country, as collected by a Belgian, Jacques de Beuque.

After a visit to a museum, perhaps a walk. There are plenty of green open spaces and places to take exercise within the city boundaries. And a walk on one of the Floresta da Tijuca tropical rainforest trails would certainly be an exercise. But with its monkeys and its sloths, the park is highly popular, especially at weekends. Not only the largest urban park in Brazil, it is the largest in the world, occupying an area of nearly 13 square miles (3,300 hectares), enabling city-dwellers to come close up to endangered plants and animals. Scenic viewpoints, dells and lakes, and the 100-foot (30-meter) high Taunay waterfall, visible from quite a few of the more than 200 trails, account for the popularity of the park. But caution is required. It is not difficult for a visitor to get lost – even within sight of Rio's high-rise buildings on the horizon.

The park has been designated a protected biotopic zone by UNESCO.

Rio's botanical gardens sprawl over an area of 247 acres (one-third of a square mile, 100 hectares), contain some 5,000 different plant species, and provide another quiet spot in which to get away from the hustle and bustle of the city. An impressive avenue of palm trees planted in 1842 provides the entrance to the gardens created in 1808. The first trees in the gardens were planted the following year by command of the regent Dom João VI himself. Ancient trees, orchids and water-lilies flourish in wondrous peacefulness.

Close by is Lagoa Rodrigo de Freitas, a roughly semicircular lake that is a favorite spot for locals. A nature reserve since 1986, it has excellent paths for jogging along, and open areas for soccer matches. Its shores provide a pleasantly calm atmosphere encouraging visitors to relax and reenergize before again plunging into the heady social whirlwind that is Rio.

Among other museums, the International Museum of Naïve Art has much to recommend it. It opened in 1995, and contains 8,000 works of art from around 100 different countries. Reckoned to be the largest work of naïve art in the world, at 13 x 23 feet (4 x 7 meters), a painting by the Rio artist Lia Mittarakis is one of the featured exhibits. It is a colossal work endeavoring to immortalize her city on canvas. It is also practically priceless. Smaller, lesser works, however, are for sale in the museum shop. The museum is housed within an old villa next to the lower terminus of the funicular railway up the Corcovado.

52. Frontages in the Largo do Boticario.

53. Frontages in the Largo do Boticario.

But Rio is full of museums. There is, for example, the Museu da Chácara do Céu in the artists' quarter, Santa Teresa, which has a fine reputation and is almost crammed with works of art. Surrounded by valuable pieces of furniture are original paintings by such artists as Monet, Picasso and Dalí. The museum also offers sightseers excellent views over Guanabara Bay – particularly of the Sugarloaf – from its windows.

And then there is the Museu de Arte Moderna (MAM), perhaps the best show-place for modern art in the whole of South America. It suffered a disastrous fire in 1979, in which nearly 1,000 irreplaceable works of art were lost, including pieces by Miró, Picasso and Paul Klee. But it reopened in 1990, and now contains some 4,000 works, a fair number of which are by the museum's founder, Gilberto Chateaubriand.

If you can't resist spending your money and want to buy something pricey and worth keeping, you could do much worse than visit Ipanema where, in some of the better streets, Rio's most expensive jewelers have their shops. Hans Stern's shops are world-famous: he is the largest jeweler in the city. In his main store Stern offers a guided tour to the different workshops in which rough, unpolished rocks are turned into exquisitely-set pieces of jewelry. The store even has its own museum. It was in 1939 that the German-born Stern emigrated to Rio and started up the enterprise that now owns 170 shops in twelve countries.

67. The International Museum of Naïve Art.

preceding pages
68. The Laranjeiras district.

69. The church of Nossa
    Senhora da Glória.
70. The church of Nossa
    Senhora da Glória by night.
71. Blue-tiled decoration in the
    church of Nossa Senhora da
    Glória.

A flashing gemstone might inspire any girl to party. And the people of Rio know how to party! Not just at Carnival time. Not just when the Brazilian national soccer team has won. No – all Rio goes utterly crazy every year on New Year's Eve as well, when some $2^{1/2}$ million people flock to Copacabana beach in honor of Yemanjá, goddess of the sea. For the locals, this is the greatest religious festival of all. They put their best clothes on, construct small altars out of fruits and flowers, and light thousands of candles. And as the waves wash upon the shore, the faithful pray or walk into the water to cast a bunch of gladioli onto its undulating surface.

Preceding pages

72. The Old City Palace, formerly the Imperial Palace.

73. Frontages at Ipanema.

74. Gentleman of the road taking his ease near the park, Ipanema.

75. Stained-glass window depicting Emperor Pedro II, on the island of Iscal.

The beautiful and the fit in Rio

Forever dreaming of Pelé . . .

92. Maracaña Stadium.

93. Maracaña Stadium.

94. Maracaña Stadium.

If there is a god of soccer, his worship stems from Brazil. The people are all crazy about soccer. It ranks immediately after Carnival – perhaps even before it – perhaps both are of equal ranking – no one can say. It affects people's lives. It takes them emotionally to the heights or to the depths. They live and breathe soccer.

And their greatest hero of all is Pelé (born Edson Arantes do Nascimento in 1940). Even today, in his sixties, Pelé is a cultural icon. Every boy in Rio knows of him and wants to do what he has done. Very few ever get close. But hope reigns supreme among the young soccer players on the beaches and in the dim back streets. It would be one way to leave the misery, the poverty, for ever and to join the world of glamor, of filmstars and starlets . . . never again to be hungry . . . to be surrounded by beautiful women, to have money to burn . . . to be like those more modern soccer superstars Bebeto, Ronaldo, Romario . . .

The 1970s soccer star Zico now has his own soccer school in Rio, where boys train until they drop.

Soccer is all-important in Brazil. Even more so in Rio, which has the world's largest stadium – the Maracaña – a huge sports complex surrounded by practice fields and training facilities. No fewer than 199,854 spectators in the Maracaña watched Brazil play Uruguay in its inauguration year, 1950. Brazil might have lost that game – but no other nation has won the World Cup so many times. A goal in the Maracaña, and the occupants of the cheaper seats go wild. Ecstatic frenzy! The samba drums throb as if they will never stop.

95. Maracaña Stadium.
96. Football anywhere and
    everywhere.

Young lads in Rio kick a football around whenever they can, wherever they are, whether at the campo ('pitch') in the Morro dos Prazeres favela, with its background panorama of the famous Sugarloaf mountain or in the red-hot sands of Copacabana beach (where the floodlights are turned on for spectators from afternoon until late evening). If they are good, they may be spotted. If they are spotted they may have it made. Soccer stars in Brazil are like pop stars or filmstars in other countries. People from the poorest backgrounds can elevate themselves from the lowest depths of society to the ultimate heights – and be idolized for it – like Romario.

Rio's top soccer club is Flamengo. Zico played for Flamengo from the age of 15. Now the club has some 20 million registered local fans, of a team that has been the champions of Rio more than twenty times. Nationwide, the club has 35 million fans. On the rare occasions the team loses, Rio goes into deep mourning. For a time the mood of the city is just like at the end of Carnival.

97. Samba buffs.

Zico's soccer school is situated in the rather fashionable suburb of Barra. It works on an unusual philosophy. Around 100 boys from the slum areas train free of charge – which is not only an honorable gesture on the school's part but sends out a ray of hope to many talented children who would not otherwise have a chance to progress. Moreover, the school retains strong links with the Flamengo club, and has been known to place its best players in the club directly.

Those who join the club are definitely on the way up. The benefits of lesser fame with the prospects of greater fortune. It is a scenario familiar to those who appreciate the somewhat exhibitionist nature of Brazilians in general and of Rio's citizens in particular. Most people live their lives as if they were permanently under the spotlight, many also keeping up grueling fitness training regimes accordingly. Rio is the fitness capital of the world: it has more than 300 registered keep-fit centers, and doubtless some unregistered. Torture chambers in which muscles are toned to steel, not so much for reasons of health as to be able to bask in other people's admiration of a well-proportioned body. Everyone in Rio wants to be admired, and especially for the way they look. The body is an asset toward this. Not surprisingly, then, Rio is blessed with an enormous number of resident plastic surgeons – possibly more of them than there are hospital physicians. And plastic surgery there is not too expensive, or so the patients say. Liposuction to remove tummy spread or breast implants to improve the figure are available for a modest $2,000 to $3,000. A full face-lift costs rather more – $2,500 to $4,000 – although a simple nose-job would set you back a mere $1,500 to $2,000.

Every favela, every little community within a favela, every school within a community has its own annual beauty contest. The body beautiful is a body happy. Women frantically straighten their hair using all kinds of potentially harmful unguents. Skin-care preparations are used massively. It is beauty first and foremost. The Church has long since given up trying to dislodge concern for the physical body from its primary position. All this combined with the custom in Rio for tactile conversations. People kiss each other on saying hello and goodbye – even those who are meeting for the first time. What might be construed elsewhere in the world as little less than sexual harassment is only good manners in Rio. 'Humans are the first animals in creation to discern the aesthetic,' Ivo Pitanguy (the world-famous plastic surgeon) has said, 'and the quest for beauty is a human right.' Now there's a man who knows his value to the world.

Well, if as a man you can't be beautiful you can at least become a famous soccer-player and earn lots of money. Then it doesn't matter all that much what you look like. People will worship you anyway. So long as you score good-looking goals.

98. The fitness cult takes many
different forms .

The world's most famous sandbox

Copacabana: the place to see and be seen

101. Aerial view of Rio de Janeiro, showing the beaches of Copacabana and Ipanema.

99. Volleyball on Copacabana beach.

100. Rollerskating at Copacabana.

It is Sunday morning. The sun is not all that hot for the moment – the temperature is around 68°F (20°C) – and a slight breeze blows gently. There is still room to sit on one of the stone seats close to the Copacabana. The beach has not filled up yet. But it is the calm before the storm. The whole of Rio spends Sunday at the Copacabana, the most famous sandbox of the world. In an hour or so it will be impossible to find a vacant spot anywhere on the beach.

But at this moment, while half of Rio is having its breakfast (or perhaps coming home after a night out at the disco), most of the people visible on the beach are there because they are paid to be – life-guards, swimming instructors, or men renting out deckchairs or volleyball nets – or joggers and serious athletes out exercising their well-toned bodies of a morning.

For Brazilians, a presence at the Copacabana is mandatory for one thing only: to be seen. The Brazilian population in general – currently some 170 million strong – believe themselves to be the most beautiful people on Earth, and the beach is the place to prove it. There the men can show off their steely muscles, the total absence of fat, the 'pecs' and the 'six-packs' as if they were on a catwalk. Nowhere is the body cult so marked as it is at the Copacabana. And no one would dream of reading a book (or doing anything else so trite) while these lords of creation publicly indulge in power-walking, body-building ... and amatorial dalliance. There they go, in their shades and their tight little swim trunks, winking every so often at the ladies. The ladies in turn whip out their lipsticks from their G-string bathing suits and gaze into their handheld mirrors with a charmingly blasé expression on their faces. It is all a ritual.

102. Sand sculptures on Copacabana.

103. Sunbathing on Barra beach.

104. Barra da Tijua.

The taut backsides and the minute bathing suits – the 'floss bikinis', as the locals call them – are legendary. See and be seen … and, if the opportunity should present itself, go a little further. That is the motto at Rio's world-famous beach.

It's a colorful way of life. Even those without money in their pockets stay cheerful. Here at the beach, the only thing that counts is whether you are young and whether you can do 20 pushups in a row or keep the soccer ball from touching the ground without using your hands. The boy or man who can is king – no matter whether he sleeps in a well-appointed mansion at night or dosses down under the stars. He may or may not also be a sun-worshiper – as some of them are. Well oiled, sun-worshipers tend to lie absolutely statically on the beach, their bodies oriented in the appropriate direction, staring, persevering, patient. And besides the sun-worshipers, there are the voodoo buffs. These stay close to a wine-bottle with a candle stuck in the top that they have buried in the sand, ready and waiting for anything that may come. The beach has its fair share of weirdos and crazies.

Now it is midday. The sun over Rio is burning hot – 100°F (38°C) in the shade. But that doesn't stop the volleyball freaks from having a fast and furious game. These athletes of near-professional standards may in fact be bank clerks or real estate executives or janitors – but what they do for a living interests nobody when they are on the beach. Neither on a Sunday nor on any other day. What counts is that they enjoy themselves. And that they have a lean, hard body. They play soccer, or beach tennis. Some dance to samba music. Children, adolescents, boys and girls chase after the inevitable soccer ball through the ankle-deep sand – it is one of the best forms of muscle training there is. Here and there the barefoot beach vendors set up their stalls and sell cool beer in cans. Or if alcohol is not your tipple today, you can buy coconut milk instead.

105. Surf at Ipanema.

106. Surf at Ipanema

The beach has something for everybody. The white sand is part of life, and the people of Rio cannot imagine life without it. The obsession with it may even have historical roots. In 1808 the Portuguese regent João was obliged by the advance of Napoleon to flee his own country, but in escaping was bitten by a tick. His doctors advised him that he needed to swim in the ocean daily. His daily visit to the beach thereafter may have inspired a national institution. Certainly, for almost all Rio residents, at the weekend and during vacations the day is divided into the time before going to the beach and the time after going to the beach.

But of course, Copacabana is by no means Rio's only beach. The upper echelons of society generally prefer to sunbathe at Ipanema, to the west, where filmstars and starlets congregate. Then there is Leblon beach, farther west still. The locals here are wealthy, and the sands are turned into something of a catwalk, particularly at weekends. The longest beach of all is the Barra da Tijuca: 13 miles (20 kilometers) of clean sand that is regarded as especially fashionable – and so is the meeting-place of the young.

107. Ipanema beach.

Rio's beaches provide considerable study material for amateur sociologists, as well as excellent ideas and themes for fine arts buffs in the literary, theater and music scenes. Motifs are always changing. Intellectuals in Paris may visit their cafés, aesthetes in Rio visit a beach. But essentially, the sands are a prime means of escape for millions of citizens. Indeed, one rather patronizing view is that the free availability of the beaches is a major factor in keeping the residents of the shanty towns, the favelas, fairly peaceably reconciled to their desperate poverty. Few people ever think in such terms. After all, it would seem that no one at all has bothered to wonder how reconciled (let alone happy) the small number of fishermen that go out in their fishing-boats from the western end of the Copacabana are with their lot, as they foray out into the cold Atlantic most days.

108. Looking out to sea from Arpoador beach.

109. The fishermen anticipating a net profit.

110. The fishermen returned from fishing.

In view of the importance of the beaches to most of the people of Rio, however, it is not surprising that local politicians have from time to time attempted to make use of them in their campaigns. One promising presidential candidate in the 1980s, for example, received considerable support after he set up a bus service from downtown to the beaches. It is not everyone who lives close to a beach.

Even less surprising is the fact that those who do live close enough tend to ask themselves one and the same question day after day: 'Will the weather be good on the beach tomorrow?' They needn't bother themselves. The answer is always Yes.

The beach is a way of life in itself. It is also a mirror of society. Some have doubted that Einstein could have developed his theories of relativity had he lived close to the Copacabana. Accredited workaholics have been known to be 'cured' by the sunshine on the sands. And many a previously lethargic and overweight desk-jockey from the multitudinous offices in Rio has been turned into a finely honed athlete.

But you will have to get up early if you like seclusion while you are doing the honing, running your distance in the world's most famous sandbox. Especially on a Sunday.

City in frenzy
Carnival time in Rio

111. Carnival parades around
the Sambodrom.

112. Carnival parades around
the Sambodrom.

113. Carnival parades around
the Sambodrom.

A mass of color. A throng of interweaving humanity. Flying arms, trailing headdresses, wafting skirts. Loud music to the throb of drums. Magnificently decorated floats, and scantily clothed people. If there is one event that Rio is uniquely famous for, it is Carnival. It centers on Shrove Tuesday every year. It happens in Rio. And there is nothing else like it in the world.

Because there is nothing else like it, it is as fantastic an experience every time. Nowhere else is such an effort put into celebrating a festival. For what else would some people save up to 50 percent of their annual wages just to have the pleasure of blowing it away over four frenetic days? For what else would others spend evening after evening undergoing torture in the samba schools after a hard day's work all in the vague hope of perhaps winning a prize?

And certainly, Carnival in Rio has little in common with the Mardi Gras in Europe, whether or not there are exuberant parties involved, with singing and dancing and swaying to rhythmic music. That only lasts for one afternoon, or at most, a couple of nights. No – above all, Carnival in Rio is brutally competitive. Prizes are awarded by juries for such essential qualities as best-designed costume, most elaborate costume, most well-chosen music, and most appropriate choreography. And to impress the jury, groups make their preparations and rehearse for maybe the whole of the previous eleven months. Dance steps are practiced in countless repetition; the costumes are designed, cut out and stitched together; the songs are written and their words are learned up. Nothing is left to chance. Thousands go to one or other of the samba schools to be sure of getting it right on the night.

At last it is time to go to the Sambodrom, Rio's largest Carnival stadium, which cost some 23 million US dollars to build, and which holds around 85,000 spectators. This is where the decisions will be made. This is where, group by group, thousands parade in front of a passionate audience. Precision and discipline are the essentials. Every musician and dancer must know his or her role exactly. The drums beat, and the heat and the music envelop the stadium. Even the most tone-deaf flat-footed spectator eventually succumbs to the magic of Carnival.

114-117. Carnival parades
around the
Sambodrom.

For the juries, the parade is organized as if all competitors were in a conference or league – with a first, a second, and a third division. For each division the judges evaluate the quality and the originality of the performance of each school. Different schools have their own fans (the torcedores) in the audience. Of course the samba schools are immensely gratified when some Brazilian celebrity expresses his or her support for them – and even more if he or she actually attends classes.

Yet tourists who come to Rio for nothing else than the Carnival may go away disappointed. 'Carnival', according to the locals, 'is the art of living', and includes communicating one's feelings. For those who speak no Portuguese, that communication may be lacking, and they may quickly feel themselves isolated within the throbbing multitude. Audience participation is (and has to be) wholehearted; they are all one with the dancers and musicians at the center of the stage. This is the crux of the difference between Rio's Carnival and 'carnivals' in Europe, where spectators can remain passive observers if that is what they want.

And it has to be said that criminal elements take advantage of the giant street festival when and where they can, samba or no samba. Pickpockets flourish and proliferate. Crooked gambling joints enjoy an annual boom. Just as dishonestly, perhaps, hotel prices leap dramatically during Carnival, and bar and restaurant prices go through the roof (as everyone knows they will). An expensive business – that is, Carnival can be expensive for some, good business for others.

But the locals care little about the financial aspects. It is Carnival they love. For them it is the most significant event in Brazilian life, and they therefore also love to see it reflected as such in Brazilian literature. So the novelist Jorge Amado is regarded as having paid the ultimate compliment to Carnival (and hence to the Brazilian way of life) by titling one of his popular books Country of Carnival. Many Brazilian poets have used the Carnival as a metaphor for Brazil itself. In the early years of the 20th century, Olavo Bilac described the Carnival fanatic (the Carnevalesco) thus: he or she 'is fundamentally different from other people, and indeed belongs to a quite independent species'. The Carnevalesco is not a person who just enjoys the Carnival – he or she lives and breathes Carnival. The only regret at death for the Carnevalesco is that he or she will no longer be able to go on celebrating the Carnival.

So the Carnival in Rio is not at all the same as the Mardi Gras celebrations in Europe. Yet what takes place in the streets of Rio has its origins across the Atlantic. The derivation of the word carnival nonetheless remains obscure. Most likely it comes fairly directly from Latin and means no more than '(festival of) meat', referring to the feasting of Shrove Tuesday before the fasting of Ash Wednesday and Lent. The folk-etymology is that it derives from Latin Carne vale, 'O meat, farewell!', with much the same reference in mind anyway.

It was in the late 19th century that people of non-European ancestry were allowed to participate in the Carnival for the first time. There was a serious drought in the northeastern part of Brazil in 1877, which caused many black people, some of them slaves, to migrate to Rio. With them they brought their own forms of music and dance, and at Carnival time were not shy of making them public as they tried to forget their poverty. After all, the point of Carnival for most of Rio's citizens has always been communal pleasure involving boisterous merrymaking and dancing, with copious amounts of alcoholic beverage. For the middle and upper classes, however, the boisterousness and the alcohol are not at all so essential. The point of Carnival for them is they they should let their

hair down, lose their inhibitions, for a period (though probably not for four whole days). This is why Carnival time in some households of Rio is celebrated only with uncomplicated folk music played on simple instruments.

118. A line in sequins and spangles.

119. Carnival-dancer from Bahia having a good time in the street.

For others, Carnival represents the complete reversal of the everyday. Whatever is important for the rest of the year has no significance at all during Carnival. Catholic morals? Forget them. Society's barriers between black and white, rich and poor? What barriers? There are no restrictions. The city goes mad, and enjoys going mad. Mario Vargas Llosa, the famous South American author, has written:

During a brief moment of impossible fantasy involving a fixation with sex and rhythmic music, princesses have warts and street-sweepers are blond and handsome; beggars are benevolently happy and millionaires the soul of misfortune; plain girls are wondrously pretty, and beautiful girls take your breath away completely.

The number of heart attacks in elderly men is recorded as reaching a peak at Carnival time. And in recent years the government has for obvious reasons at this time of the year distributed millions of condoms and funded enormous AIDS awareness campaigns.

At Carnival time, illusion may be in the eye of the beholder, then, but some illusions are definitely intentional. Not all of the women are in fact female: some are men dressed up. But so what? Among the flying arms, trailing headdresses, wafting skirts, and the throbbing insistence of the samba rhythm – who cares?

120. Everyone makes their preparations to join in Carnival.

121. Carnival time.

122. Carnival time.